MEDITATIONS
ON THE ONENESS

Ken Jones

To Nelson Jesus Barquet-a great friend and influence in spiritual discussions in my life- and his youngest brother Dr. Glenn Barquet who recently passed away of COVID-19

Intro

I came to the realization within the last few years that my entire creative life has been a search for God in all forms-grace, faith, truth, sin, evil, good, reasons for the seemingly random. My current conclusion is at the essence of existence is an unknowable mystery. Physicists now say as many as ten or more universes may exist, that ours is flat or at the extreme may be a hologram in an inter-dimensional impermanence.

So my poetry is like the teenage kid who keeps rebelling, never cleans his room, doesn't give a damn what anyone thinks about me as I lunge ludicrously at questions humans are likely never meant to answer. But at least it keeps me busy. I realize now that every read and unread, and heard and unheard, word I've ever written has been my way of seeking meaning in what I thought was a meaningless universe. I hope these poems add some insight to your own vision quest.

Poet Ken Jones

TEXAS USA, 2020

"Be sure mind's nature is groundless voidness/Your mind is insubstantial like empty space-/Like it or not, look at your own mind!" The Natural Liberation Through Naked Vision Identifying Intelligence by Padma Sambhava from Essential Tibetan Buddhism trans. Robert Thurman

Contents

DEAR LOST SOUL 9

BEINGS VISIBLE AND INVISIBLE 10

MIND'S EYE 11

WHY IS ALL I AM ASKING YOU 12

ALIEN EAR HURT 13

THE BODY CYBERCOSMIC 14

ESCHATOLOGY VILLANELLE 15

WHAT'S LEFT AFTER DEATH 16

BLACKEN YOUR BLOODY I 17

NOT DEAD YET 18

BIZARRE OR BALANCED? 19

DERVISH WISH 20

HE IS PAGING"IN THE CITY OF GOOD HEALTH, I AM
AGING"-LI QUIANGZHAO-CHINA 12TH CENTURY 21

DIM LEMMINGS 22

SPIRIT SPOKEN 23

SACRED GEOMETRY 24

THE VALUE ADDED TAXES OF SIN 25

SPARKLING AIR WORMS 26

FROM CRIMSON SHAME 27

KILL NOT A FLY 28

PRAYER #3 29

THE FAMILY TREE 30

KULA SUNSET (FOR STEPHEN LUKSIC) 31

SPEAKING TRUTH (FOR MAUI CALVIN) 32

PRISON LANGUAGE FOR CYNTHIA MATZKE 33

FINALLY UNDERSTANDING DRESSAGE 34

FOR THE IDLE IDES OF JULY 35

BLESSINGS THROUGH THE YEARS 36

HOLD SWAY 37
MEDICINE MEMO 38
INEBRIATION 39
YOU'RE NOTHING BUT A DRUNKEN BUM! 40
THE PEACOCK ANGEL (FOR THE GENOCIDED YEZIDI) ..41
JUMPING JACK FLASH HYPOTHESIS 43
A LIFE OF DISAGREEMENT 44
TO THE DEFIANT DEAF CHILDREN 45
MIND EXPANSION VIA TOLERANCE 46
GOD IS REAL 47
BEYOND THE QUANTUM CHOICE 48
THE UNIVERSE IS A QUANTUM COMPUTER 49
CYBERSPACE HYPERNAUTS I 50
VICTORIOUS INTERNET II 51
PAGE REVEALED 52
MISSION IMPOSSIBLE 53
TRIOLET OF NEW LIFE FORCE 54
BUBBLE OF NOTHING 55
MENTAL YOGA 56
THEY LIVE/ LYING SMILING REPTILES 57
GOD, NATURE, AND MOTHER EARTH 58
GOD LOVES SEX AND DEATH 59
THE MEANING OF LIFE 60
ASPIRE NO HIGHER 61
DEITY TODAY 62
JOURNEY'S END 63
A NEW REASON TO CARE 65
NEVER GOOD ENOUGH 68

DEAR LOST SOUL

Ignorance winks at your devices
The Godhead isn't gold or stone
Listen as you sit alone
To the small still voice inside

Idols are the works of human hands
The Godhead isn't glass or plastic
See as you fight your blindness
The Light fills your Holy sick

Tradition offers this decision
The Godhead's Invisible throne
Taste its essence before death
Confess, do good, Omniscience's breath

Omnipotent moments in this powerless time
The Godhead permeates all zones
Touch the words in the Book of Life
Survive unimaginable strife

Nearing the unvarnished finish
The Godhead hides in a burnt dish
Smell the ashes of this hellish realm
Relinquish the wish for the helm

Final Analysis balances
On a beam of insatiable Spirit
Quaff quantum valences
Smell, touch, taste, see and hear it

BEINGS VISIBLE AND INVISIBLE

Substance of hope, I wait for the words
Which tell of the War of the Auroras
The Blood of Living Earth
Where scythes of lust slice fecund fields.

Ennobled stewards of the plentiful planet
Open the eyes of those who dwell in darkness
Open the mouths of those who speak only in thought
Open the ears of those who solely hear silences

In the wide sky, you understand the Great Mystery
Changes hearts in an electric jolt
A second chance to enhance each experience
As your Power flies through never dying eyes
Touches your enemies with their abrupt corruption.

The Siege of this Spirit lasts a lifetime
And ends in a heartbeat.

MIND'S EYE

And how the homeless swarm came
To symbolize souls is obvious.
Transcendence is only a desperate attempt
To master the hidden in silence.
Observation is a hominid reflex
Five senses bind our dying bodies.
Philosophical Mind is above, behind,
Beyond the temporal or is that mere human hubris?
We scoured our soul to lose this sphere
And find in Mind etched templates
Buried in synapse canyons
Here is where the Heart so abstract
Causes Mind to pause its attack
Game on hold, you contemplate
Our meaningless, not so great Fate.

WHY IS ALL I AM ASKING YOU

Praise to Spring's Saturnalia
We need the release of dishonor
Praise to the eternal debauched Mardi Gras
Leading society down the bead covered maw
Praise to the Vaginal cure of Mother Earth's embrace
Let me scream naked in a pagan dance
Shame on our way of hiding from the Light's behavior
Praise the Sun's force as the Life Spirit's savior
Hidden in gravity is the key to the stars
Shame on the shame of a contactee's scars

The transoceanic global monoculture
We praise or wish shame on its voracious vulture
In these poetic prayers all you can do is spew
Chunks of Cosmology- a Philosopher's brew
Quite stout at time-Space is askew
Why is all I am asking You

ALIEN EAR HURT

As a time of creation lists toward Starboard
The port of tomorrow hides deathly sorrow
This shout is nothing but an unheard Word
Caught in the flux of a beautiful flow

As an issue and problem become twin conundrums
The riddle's mystery is Delphic fumes
To an unsupported conclusion we come
Skirting the hurting of inchoate dooms

THE BODY CYBERCOSMIC

Here in the cacophony of silence
I found a spirit in science
A meaning inside the violence
A will behind every triumph
Alive to the corridors of data
Synapse floods of meaning
Electric sparks enlighten the dark
William Blake and Tycho Brache
Exchange addresses in Jerusalem
Misspelled spiritual capitals
Leave Mohammed off the list.
A death sentence is always on us
So sorry, worry need not interest me
Foucault said it best when coherent
Not at the edge of a bondage whip
Wherefore are thou, Romeo?
In a cock's head in Borneo?
In a pale white vaginal tornado?
In a hand at the end of Figaro?
Weak as the knees I crawl on
Barking like a disenfranchised pawn
I sing the body cybercosmic
Then laugh as it's all so comic.

ESCHATOLOGY VILLANELLE

This world will end the day you breathe your last
Pray to your meager deities-they laugh
Time present and time future are time past

You witches with the pagan spells you cast
Channel evil spirits though the Devil's staff
The world will end the day you breathe your last

Though Mayan ruins argue Time's not vast
Your prophecy is proven as a gaffe
Time present and time future are time past

Or will Jesus Christ return so fast
You sip his blood from a holy chalice
This world will end the day you breathe your last

Crane your neck to heaven like a giraffe
Bury your snout in hell like poor riff raff
Time present and time future are in time past
This world will end the day you breathe your last

WHAT'S LEFT AFTER DEATH

Flooding the bloodstream of consciousness, dots of harm float past placidly like amoeba on slides or sea horses in shallow waters-nets bereft of craft catch blasts of poetic attack-a life raft or shaft-daft as the fact I keep pouring piffle on these pages-my mental stages where my rage at Adam failure can sail unassaulted by pole vaulted exalted palsied palaver. Guess who, what, or where your next care will come from? Dumb, Dumb,Dumb, numb in a tub-Aye, there's the club-a dub of Ascended Masters' disaster precursors-why did I strive to stay alive though these etchings and scratchings-to start screaming. I pretend it will outlast me but my dead friends are proof that when you're gone the world carries on and may pay no attention to what you spent your existence creating-it was always a futile race against an inevitable clock but it's ultimate worthlessness hurts worse than the pains of its birth-Dearth is your last breath's girth

BLACKEN YOUR BLOODY I

Weakened by weary wasteling wandering
I stumble from bottle to bar and back again
Disabled by too much ability
Sickened by premature senility
Appalling Gestalt halts in serious sin

Twitches in my eye reveal no revelation
Electricity currently in reliever polarity position
Shocked by diversity insulation
No one tells me what to do
Or what to feel or why

I'll blacken your Bloody I
Everything you write is a lie

NOT DEAD YET

I found God's grace
In my darkest sin
The mystery has no face
You only see It within

In my dirty body
Was a holy brain
My hands were bloody
From an inner stain

Dead to the world
Dead to all flesh
I awake in sacred pearls
Reborn and refreshed

To my Brothers and Sisters in Spirit
Open your eyes to hear it
Open your ears to see it
Open your hearts to spear it

No more work!
No more property!
Is it blasphemy?
Is it heresy?
Or are we finally free!

BIZARRE OR BALANCED?

I praise what is forbidden
Seeking Sparks of Divinity
In polluted husks hidden
My winning sets them free

Your holy books are bullshit
My wife is a sacred whore
You simpletons sit and spin
Dervish prophets keep score

Transgression sanctified
Redemption purified
Universal Light I ride
Good and Evil smile allied

DERVISH WISH

If God is love
As Rumi spoke
Let Spirit emote

To whirl is divine
Let arms entwine
Then reach for sky

Yet one hand must
Face the dust
So Power flows down

Bridge the unseen
We exist between
The Perfect's hidden stream

Feint toward Light
Live Illumined insight
Faint in fright

HE IS PAGING"In the City of Good Health, I am aging"-Li Quiangzhao-China 12th Century

In the City of Good Health, I am aging
My spirit slows still the fuse stays lit
Though my temples gray, my heart is raging

My spirit slows as my fuse stays lit
Distant ancestors, lost friends paging
Gaps of life between my will and wit

Though my temples gray, my heart is raging
To rise against I now must calmly sit
In the City of Good Health, I am aging

Awaiting the next Revolution, I quit
Though my temples gray, my heart is raging
My Decadence and Death Mask barely fit

So the Director in charge of the staging
Has reasons why he is now engaging
Though my temples gray, my heart is raging
In the City of Good Health, I am aging

DIM LEMMINGS

"Each new hour holds new chances/For new beginnings" Maya
Angelou

Behind the wall the mass prosperous
Fattened comfort junkies consume
Digital streams, Bit Torrent dreams
Though food riots hit Invisible Others
Dim lemmings for Gaia's trimming
In what foul selfish pools we're swimming!
The Y chromosomes bringing war home
Loving X could save
but Lysistrata's in her grave
Twisted genetic strands
are xenophobic brands
We are an Alien's holy cattle
Now our Minds must battle
Rise above the coding
But like a calf at a roping
Those impulses pull us to dust
Our legs bound in seconds
By the cowboy of callous selfishness
Who lives buried deep within each of us

SPIRIT SPOKEN

See the face of God in a Mother
Signing off key praises to its name
A drunken Friday night
On a vomit blood stained futon
A homeless woman hand outstretched
In front of a rich suburban Xmas service
An AIDS victim holding a sign
In the middle of Western Avenue
A thunderstorm with violent lightning
Lighting a West Texas plain
A heightened flash when the word
"Spirit" is spoken

SACRED GEOMETRY

Stones placed first this way
Then spiraled on the paths
Mortared angles symmetry
Delicately balances lathes
Mind finds openness
Spirit revived in stages
Temples for eternal truth
Walking the labyrinth

We are casualties of history
Spirit quieted by science

THE VALUE ADDED TAXES OF SIN

She groveled toward the wistful warden
With an absinthe decanter.
Her bloodied knees floated on a Ouija Board
Because mystery messages enchanted her.
The warden, while juggling cabbages,
Bifurcated her head with a blunt stone
She laughed as if happy her open skull
Showed only Gray matter, not bare bone
Two guards barbed into the infirmary
"She fell" muttered the warden with a sideways grin
"We won't tell" mutters the burly state troopers
Call it the Value Added Taxes of Sin

SPARKLING AIR WORMS

Robotic Reticulum, ordered from the void
To build a message and a dream
As He is Him, and we are in the sun
Whether we know it or not is how it seems

To seem is a seam on the cosmic beam
Ceiling sky's painted pained mystery
To ride a Reticulum tomb as the Moon screams
At the cornea cortex of the pyramid's eye

Why and why, sick psychotic pressed Humans
You see we build a message, then swim
In the uncertain ocean of creation
We are in the sun, and He is Him

FROM CRIMSON SHAME

Never facing how we all are to blame
Society takes a collective nap
Until our eyes glow crimson with the shame

Loss is our golf partner-scratch handicap
Never facing how we all are to blame
Every encounter holds another trap

Until our eyes glow crimson with the shame
Into some core of shared feelings we tap
Never facing we all are to blame

We sip Spirit's now bitter viscous sap
Until our eyes glow crimson with the shame
The only poultice for our dead soul's gap

Can we now all follow Great Spirit's map?
Return the tribal healing to our lap?
Finally facing how we all are to blame
Freeing our eyes' glow from crimson shame

KILL NOT A FLY

The curtain between my certain self
And everything threatens to tear
Hurting is a daily wave I surf
And nothing is a bathrobe I wear
No distance separates yours and my turf
Anything is beyond where I stare
The layered wood, the liquor shelf
And everything I've drunk on there

Harm your karma beyond human help

PRAYER #3

One Presence
One Power
One Infinite Love
May Forgiveness Clear Consciousness
Surrender All Resentments and Condemnations
Reject All Hostile Mental Turmoil
Receive Clean Energy
Return to Cosmic Harmony

THE FAMILY TREE

The promiscuous bonobo and altruistic macaque
Led the primate counter attack
The vegetarian gorilla and nurturing baboon
Prayed Change would come soon
The feces throwing rhesus and fairy chimpanzee
Joined in with hopeful glee
On one fact they all agree:
Human hierarchy ruins the family tree

KULA SUNSET (for Stephen Luksic)

Ecosystem Instability
Meet Flash Mob Sustainability
Primate Inability
Masked as Ingenuity
Species careening toward Naught
Skeletal skull sips Drought
Stop to savor a sunset
Slide into infinity Forget
Vog clouds your Dream Sky
Regret the eternal Why

SPEAKING TRUTH (for Maui Calvin)

"Corporations are terrorists" -Calvin on Maui

Beheading Mother Earth
Set afire her fertile fields
Spray bullets of biotech
Deadly poison yields

Evil void controls the soil
Enslaves germinating seeds
Repetitive genetic toil
Feed these barbarians' greed

Can the People seize the Power
In this fateful final hour
Or will the hole in Capital's soul
Swallow our species whole?

PRISON LANGUAGE for Cynthia Matzke

Your sing song melodies of freedom
Have soured into the click clack scrape
Of bottle nose teeth across iron bars

Your cage is a circus aquarium
Where the truly dumb humans
Force performances on your warm forms

Your angry language radiates
In subsonic waves of aquatic angst
Deaf to the Nazi primate guards

Your pain vibrates the antennae of my soul
My disdain for my speciesist shackles plain
As prisoners of conscience we both remain

FINALLY UNDERSTANDING DRESSAGE

Lippanzer stallions lead a lonely life
Bred from birth by Austrian Eugenics
Their first few years they run brown wild
On Syrian plains utterly unfettered
Cultivating a frolicking Spirit
Then suddenly a trainer seizes them
Secretly serving his Master's mission
To turn this stallion into a willing performer
Of intricate dancing, intimate prancing
Infinite romancing of the Royal audience
He performs at their commands, a hidden order
Handed down for centuries by all participating parties
In ancient leather binders
Finally entwined seemingly in their DNA
The chosen ones reproduce-barely sniffing
Their mate then quickly return to the stage.
The luckiest live in grand style for 20 years
Befitting a noble, doomed creature

FOR THE IDLE IDES OF JULY

Rising I drain my bladder
　In me is a sacred ladder
If the Gods smile I empty my bowels
　Not on sheets or tile or towels
Then I break my fast again
　Lack of food the greatest sin
Finding a trifle for my mind
　If the Gods are feeling fine
I have no need for toil or travail
　I own no soil nor tell no tales
So back to bed I lamely crawl
　The Gods make me repeat it all
I pray to them for some relief
　But no reward for my belief
So in my sad and lonely grief
I wait for next day's waste and beef

BLESSINGS THROUGH THE YEARS

Great Spirit sent me
A beautiful feather today
Then told me to pray.
I prayed for my lover's health
I prayed for my family's wealth
I prayed these wishes in stealth
Then I stood to shout a Psalm
Nestled in my clenched palm
But decided to stay calm.
At that moment a breeze arose
A deaf woman struck a pose
My shallow soul froze
A message zapped my toes.
Great Spirit bears all our fears
Every beer poured in our tears
Friends, enemies, strangers, dears,
Blessings through the years

HOLD SWAY

I stayed in the house where the Dalai Lama does
Because the people were stealing from the temple
When will they learn
This lesson so simple:
Let Great Spirit hold sway.

I lived in a house in the Hollywood Hills
All my luck made me feel ill
When I thought they had trapped me
The Spirits came and zapped me
To Let Great Spirit hold sway

When you think your soul is lost
On an ocean violently tossed
Spirits arrive to show you who's boss
Then the holding sway never goes away

A vagabond man with an Earth renewal plan
A homeless bum at home everywhere
Mother Earth's waiting
Her breath poised and bated
For the children again to care
Let Great Spirit hold sway
The Sacred Life won't have to go away

MEDICINE MEMO

The powers and ways are given to us
To pass on to others in selflessness
We get more by giving
To lose them is why we're living
As Dallas Chief Eagle discussed.

Fools Crow, like other medicine men,
Asked Black Elk to record the religion.
To share this sacred lore
Is what we're living for
Enough now of the preparation!

We agree what the Creator wants
Is, as the Higher Powers hunt,
To carry in your bones
The Spirit that heats the stones
Speak no more until you've done it.

INEBRIATION

"My feelings will warm before I drown in drink" LiQingzhao-China-12th Century

But a shot doesn't hurt!

Pit of stomach needs coals
Brow needs sweat
Hole in heart wants glow

New day loved in Death's shadow
Old wounds lost, new friends found
Present soul to drown unknown

Praise pondering what it's worth

YOU'RE NOTHING BUT A DRUNKEN BUM!

"The poor of the world are crying out"-Ariel Dorfman

He stands with the eyes of God on the corner
You ignore him
He asks with the voice of the prophets for change
You deplore him
He begs with the hands of the supplicant
You say you can't
He limps with the gait of the dissipated
"You Bum!" you rant.

One day when the first shall be last
By your broken form he'll pass
You'll dribble some feeble prayer from cracked lips
He'll laugh at the message you missed

THE PEACOCK ANGEL (for the genocided Yezidi)

Invisible transcendence
Descended onto the sun
As a seven rayed rainbow
Creation had begun

Seven sacred angels
One for every day
The most beautiful of All
Was in the seventh ray

The Peacock Angel
Isn't Satan
Yet on his grace we're waiting.

A substance in a pearl
Descended on a bird
Rumbling quaking Earth
The Force of Life now heard
Blue is the sky
Bluer is heaven
If you ask why
See what we've been given

Then a lump of flesh
Given seven senses
Into their lifeless forms
The light of Soul descended

Now he and she prays to the Sun
Source of life for everyone
If we remain in righteousness
We might see his likeness

JUMPING JACK FLASH HYPOTHESIS

Atmospheric Contamination Abounds
Ozone Depletion and Popping Sounds
Raging Fires and Massive Explosions
UV Genetic Destruction

Carmaggedon and Ship Apocalypse
 Biosphere and Infrastructure Collapse
Corpses in Low-Lying Areas
Animal Die-Offs and Genetic Chimeras

Unusual Vehicular Accidents
Neurological Damage and Land Subsidence
Possible Topplers and Zombie Files
Hydrogen Sulfide and Methane Stink

The hour is later than you think
Into Extinction's Hole we sink

A LIFE OF DISAGREEMENT

Sorrowful Mystery
At the heart of Spirit
I want to be the Prophet
In a Polygamist Death Cult
Making Real Profit
With a hand over fist that finally halts

I want to be the Savior
In a Capitalist Death System
A Criminal Behavior
That resists and fights for victims

Like Uncontacted Tribes
Solomon Islands wisdom
Souls of the dead
In the bodies of sharks
Mouth brooding tube words feast
Filter their flowery crown

I tried to wash a dish
Which said "You Only Live Once"
The letters washed away in my sink
God saying "Human! You're a dunce!"

Mathematics has no ethics
The underclass and upperclass
Both bound by metaphysics
The American way of fairness

TO THE DEFIANT DEAF CHILDREN

Why won't the backsliders listen?
You have promised to accompany the righteous
Whose eyes flow with a single Light
The message is here, if they'll open their ears
Cast away fears, become holy seers.
I, who once housed an ocean of doubt
Have now come about, willing to shout:
The path of tolerance and love is right
If you stand and fight, the glory of the Light
Will power you forward. Though broken in body
Spirit's clean machine, kept fine and free
Will shield your mode, as you download
The road of truth from the Oversoul.

MIND EXPANSION VIA TOLERANCE

I have trailed a thousand thoughts through muse-fed silent springs
Traded all my hours for so many unread things
This torrent of words I've preserved strangely not my own
So much lost, why alienate that last place I call home?
In these pieces of Spirit I shed like dying skin
Will some lasting essence remain or will doubt ever change?
The project of mind expansion tolerance diversity is beginning
Power to alter the future in our current way of living.
Adopt the attitude you wish to spread among sentient beings
Live it every day in the face of difficult challenges
No beginning promise made said this path was easy
Why are you here? The message, son, the message, use your
head.
They'll point at you in cars, tap their skull, now with hand on chin,
Like an open book they instruct you to join the secret society
they're in
But we don't tell everyone this part-maintain low tones, One,
Next breath's happening of Hope looks alive to new views

GOD IS REAL

I now address again in this prose poem the central question of human existence: does God exist? Currently I answer "Yes" but not in the fashion or with the "reasons" of most. God is behind and beyond reason. I found this fact not by faith but by experience. Though we live in the Natural World, that reality by itself doesn't blister the potential existence of Supernatural forces. I'm now convinced they exist. Beyond good and evil, beyond human morality. Mind open to signs can either see them or not. Call it Karma or Fate. I now side with the current radical physics idea that we humans live in a holographic universe, a kind of protoplasmic jelly of multiverses. And who is God?
God is a pissed off teenager upstairs in his filthy room playing us like a video game.

BEYOND THE QUANTUM CHOICE

Not risk averse but revenue neutral
You play dice with your life like the universe does
Each moment molded by molecular movements
Both here and beyond the quantum choice.
Hunger and thirst and
Pineal gland overstimulated-amusing ourselves to death
Every second a new image
Imagination can't hold all the pictures
We're all ADD leftover junkies
Where the image meets the eye to make life

Perhaps if we focused on other goals
Spiritual fulfillment instead of making money
The lack of classical education
Among even the allegedly educated.
I can't name 12 Greek myths
But I can spot hundreds of modern American ones.
Currently, this society
Is creating Olympian gods
For the next millennium empire.

THE UNIVERSE IS A QUANTUM COM-PUTER

Essence substance
Feeds on solo atoms
God the Programmer
Less is Moore's Law.
Uncertainty is an advantage
Heisenberg's iceberg
Infinitesimally titanic
Beyond the Fantastic.
Exploit quantum weirdness
To break the secret code
Zero/one, win/lose, true/false
Bit dichotomies on overload
Address frequency sporadically

CYBERSPACE HYPERNAUTS I

In a vortex to another universe
Crimson sun artificially shines
A Matamoros Whorehouse Hurricane blind
Into the wind your spirit unwinds

From a madcap mariachi message
Comes a uniform of prestaged sages
A Mumbai Bollywood Wi Fi High Five
Convincing my hard drive to stay alive

My base station elated at Broadband
Play with my mouse with your gentle hand
Put it in your carpal tunnel
Let the pain drain as if an ear funnel

VICTORIOUS INTERNET II

A torrent of words
Mostly unheard
A spectacle of the possible
For the always docile

A trickle of pixels
Slides modern sickles
Labor decentralized
And non hypnotized

A current of the current
Disbursed in a hurry
Without worry
With fury

PAGE REVEALED

You are trapped in a life you hate
Past acts tap Spirit-you berate
This dissipated resource empty state
Seems for some reason your Fate

Paper turns over-another page revealed
The Light a life of instant emptiness sealed
Weasel words are all you've heard and wield
Poet, musician, broke joke, all unreal

The toucan sees your spirit crying "Why?"
You've been shown and see the Masters in the Sky
They are still around-serving humble pie
You spit out the taste, hoping to fly

But your wings too crushed, too long held down
Grimace like an old unemployed clown
Who once was paid to smile instead of frown
The beauty of this day, these issues, sadness found

MISSION IMPOSSIBLE

" Oh, ever beauteous, ever friendly! tell,
Is it, in heaven, a crime to love too well?"-Alexander Pope, Elegy
to the Memory of an Unfortunate Lady, 1717

I am a crime; you know the gallows
   Where I wait for Death's breath
   Patiently with my spirit
Which seeks release in every swallow
   Of my heart, that pre-fab emporium
   Which sought out in its delirium
Freedom from insidious recidivism.

I am a failure; you know the alleys
   Where to lose unused Love
   Destroys my Soul from above
Which looks to annihilate the sensate
   Vulgar dissipation in the low street.
   Hard hearted enough never to meet
Lies told among us in defeat.

I am a shit; you won't let me watch you
   Urinate in a glorious squat
   Awash in what's what
   Posh in the throne of commode
   Morphing to another mode
Aliens on computers yak at me
Promising release when Mission Impossible
Is accomplished for the good of the terrestrial.

TRIOLET OF NEW LIFE FORCE

Conspiracies of Spirits wait to bleed
The ink, the words, this moment, what you need
Pale light, cold now, your body finally freed
Conspiracies of Spirits wait to bleed
New Life Force deep in some waiting seed
A black cat's half glance, a wind in wild weeds
Conspiracies of Spirits wait to bleed
The ink, the words, this moment, what you need

BUBBLE OF NOTHING

God is Satan
And Satan is God
The All-Seeing Eye
Spoils of the Rod
Never Blink
Sink in the Stink
Pyramid Power
Till your last Human Hour

I've lost the will to live but not strong enough
To kill myself so I guess I'm stuck

I walk in a bubble of Nothing
But my Indifference

I stay silent as the shells at the ocean's edge
Once holding living creatures

Lie, Cheat, Bully, Bully
Cycle through Life
Embrace the Strife
No remorse, no regret
Everyone else does it
Only sorry I got caught

MENTAL YOGA

Small still spirit inside
Silence is where it hides
Void groping toward outside
Human unity's flowing tide

Alight briefly like a buzzing fly
On the margins of the Always Why
Mooching like a pooch you try
To cancel Cosmos' electric eye
Yet you fry

THEY LIVE/ LYING SMILING REPTILES

They move/Heiling with electric guile
They tempt/With all things material
They attempt/To disarm the spiritual

We fight/ With Light and Right
Our might/ Flies like wild sprites

Our sight/Illuminated every night
No Fright/A Mystery School insight
Delights your Human Appetites

GOD, NATURE, AND MOTHER EARTH

Mysterious trumpets sound in the sky
Santa Claus Process is coming by
To say Bye Bye to the Hydrogen Sulfide
Mother Earth is a murdered bride

But wait! That blood on her wedding gown
Means Jesus Christ is coming to town
He's returning in bodily form
Mother Earth is too damn warm

Actually, she is way too Goddamn hot
I wanna watch her squat
Churn her dying oceans like a robot
Mother Earth forgives but never forgot

The Sixth Seal on Extinction's Wheel
Thanks Creator I can no longer feel
Our planet's breath of life we steal
Mother Earth's an Onion with a facial peel

Looks like us monkeys almost done
We bashed that bitch tight in her Honey Bum
But she survives as does Father Sun
God and Nature have always won

GOD LOVES SEX AND DEATH

Addressing why childhood Grace at dinner is absurd makes me seem the Sinner. I thank God for our food or else I'm a fool-a delusional tool of social control yet how apt is the rap that the food sits so lewd-God hates your shit and your sex, too-shame is your constant daily bread-forgive is our false passes as we forgive those who bump up against us-temptation is flesh's heir but his assign is Will? I'll believe it when I've had my fill. Probably the day I clutch my chest-so it's over and for the best-one mark of the dignity of humanity-never knowing when is your time to die-or is it worth saving that piece of cherry pie-no, girl, give it up to my tongue, help me feel I'm still young

THE MEANING OF LIFE

They say, " Go to the Light"
Then why do dreams come in the dark?
Are we creatures of spirit
Or just a random spark?
Or in the electricity
Do the souls ebb and flow
We all live here and now
But in the end where do we go?
Will we ever understand
Or is it all some torture show
By alien transdimensional beings
Who will never let most know
But if they show you the secret
You will never forget
But always regret

ASPIRE NO HIGHER

Spirits play us as violins
Wrapped in our separateness, these skins
Tight around us are loose enough
Not to choke is broken in
Cellular beeps are interstellar messages.

Cosmic sages page you
To call out the answer they planted
On this page, your tortured soul
Your placid face.

Spirits carve a crescent moon
Play a prayerful picayune tune
Over what soon becomes ruin.

You toss, turn, chew on,
New desires, now aspire, then
Go no higher.

DEITY TODAY

I pine for the Divine
Others called me mad
When I noticed signs
They were never glad

Their spirits like taphonomy
Fossilized and dead
They laughed at my theophany
Said it was all in my head

But God winks came in waves
Like fresh eyelash kisses
I'm not saying vision saves
But we all have human wishes

JOURNEY'S END

I come from my Dust Mother's tomb
To seek my Spirit Mother's womb
The Mystic Rose
The Sacred Lotus

I wander the Earth
Trapped by birth
In this dying body
Under the Bodhi tree
To find her Burning Bush

I yearn to return to my origin
Crush foolish Original Sin
Sip Ambrosia from a Golden Chalice
Swim in the Blood of Dionysus

I grow into a shaman
Praying to find my shamaness
She appears with Golden Apples
Open arms with a cobra in each fist

We strip to our naked essence
Purity awaits at the entrance
We embrace in the Life Affirming Dance

I become a Bee
Seeking to pollinate her Divine Flower
For the mead we need

I become a Bull
Seeking to penetrate my Creatrix
For the meat we need

Now I kiss the Gnosis
Alive and sanctified
Sweating out this profane physicality
Rising ecstatically into spirituality

Now I swallow this sacrament
The purple drank of infinite sweetness
Anointed with holy oil—
Sweet cane's cannabis softness

Eating the bread of the Presence
Tripping into the Great Mystery
On the sea foam of soma
Shedding this skin form

Transcendent
Ascendant
One with the Universe

A NEW REASON TO CARE

I.
As you put 1% eye drop death into your sight
I thought of tolerating all diversity
Then want better, wander like an Irish Setter
BESTED in the Glow of knowing
Like Gnostics reliving acrostics
Reverse the word for the Mystic's sake
Magik drinks Sake, Alleviates in effluvia
Which dissipates in mantra, consolidated.
Dr. Need Mudfer Corp.
Amalgamated Industrial Enterprises
Vertically Integrated Hierarchies
Mechanically Elevated Fuelless Paupers
Lazy Lacerated Lucky Le Duc's
Duck into a Booth to protect Hexes
MIXED misogyny of both sexes
Gated community offered immunity
If you need help, dial your Operator
My Operator lives in the sky
Why, Mr. Alien Eye, are you torturing me?

II
Stigmata Deterioration Inebriates a Station
Pen pulled dull as the next-door neighbors
Heater Spirit, nag the drum, we dance
We can't. So we etch abstractions-a distraction
To the concactation of Ill-fated recitation
Mediocrity, hypocrisy, byword hogwash
Teaching or learning-Market or nucleus?

Brain tormented overdosed empty Chiles
Tattooed freaky trendy hill viewed skewers
Barking answers land dismisses in handing
Long haired tone deaf mall adjusted perverts
Ipso facto, large hill Mafioso converts
Tent revival, insightful suicidal full dull men
Pretend the strokes of Light delight eyelash flash

Tortious tortured bleed screeching weird-etes
Rush. Pushes his tush in the ac-dc cathode tube
Ruben Brucelyn calls Lucky for a video-O-FU-I know u

III
As we talk amidst the scattered wreckage
You gave me a peck on the cheek
We headed out for a simple walk
And then we found the accident.
A plane crashed in an open field
"My God", you said, "This can't be real"
"If man were meant to fly, "I said
This fake metal bird wouldn't be in this field"

But where in the world were they going?
What would they do when they got there?
Mother Earth needs each spirit's help
That's reason enough to care.

But if you reason too much, the spirit leaches out
Falls on dry ground—our hard hands cracked
If all You can do is help All bring it back
That's reason enough to live on too shout

Where in the world are WE going?
What would we have heard if we'd arrived?
Mother Earth awaits our help to give It birth
To a new reason to care.

The innocent eyes of her young children
Await to be filled with this message of change
For her sake we music together continue
No matter where Spirit makes us awake

NEVER GOOD ENOUGH

We reach the end asking "what's the point?"
No more devils to battle or angels to anoint
One last appointment left to keep
In the apartment of eternal sleep
Our best was never good enough
Life beat us down-called our hopeless bluff
Cringing in the corner as she kicked us til we bled
Youthful dreams nightmares on our final bed
I prayed for a mother but only found a midwife
I prayed for a brother but only found strife
I prayed for a lover but found empty flesh
I prayed for others' wounds sweat wet and fresh
Now like a newborn baby-slick with placenta
God sentenced me to die here in absentia
Instead I reach for spirits to hear this final plea
Drowning in the darkness of this amniotic sea